Wallflower

Essays and Anecdotes for Quiet Women

Who Want to Be Heard

GG Renee Hill

I'm Not Crazy. I'm an Introvert.

Being around people can be so exhausting.

You see, I feel much more comfortable interacting with people intimately, one on one. I'm friendly but quiet; often preoccupied with my thoughts. I've probably been perceived as standoffish from time to time. It's not that I'm anti-social or don't like people, but I have to observe my environment to see what part I want to play in it. I may choose to open up or I may choose to stay on the outskirts looking in.

At the risk of putting myself in a box, I'm going to go ahead and say that I'm an introvert. I use the term to provide a frame of reference -- not an all-encompassing definition of who I am. If you're familiar with the Myers-Briggs personality test, I'm an INFP.

Psychiatrist Carl Jung introduced the concept of the introvert in his book *Psychological Types*. Jung's definition of an introvert is "wholly or predominantly concerned with and interested in one's own mental life," while the extrovert is "predominantly concerned with obtaining gratification from what is outside the self."

If ever a girl craved a self-definition, this was it for me. So many times I've doubted my sanity or thought something was wrong with me for being so socially awkward. I could be surrounded by people trying to out-talk each other and I'd be the quiet one wishing everyone would stop being so vocal and be more perceptive.

I struggle with giving access to people when it's not on my terms. I'd rather schedule a call than have someone call me unexpectedly. Confrontations put me at a disadvantage because I'm not able to take my time and process what's happening. I prefer writing to talking because it gives me the space and time to find the right words. When I talk too much I always end up feeling like I'm depleting my life force. That will either sound overdramatic to you, or it will sound like the words of a woman after your own heart.

I used to think that I was shy, but now I know that's not the case. I'm just reflective. I instinctively take measures to preserve myself in social environments. According to Susan Cain, author of *Quiet: The Power of Introverts in a World that Can't Stop Talking*, "Introverts are not necessarily shy. Shyness is the fear of social disapproval or humiliation, while introversion is a preference for environments that are not over-stimulating. Shyness is inherently painful; introversion is not."

I've been told that I appear confident and outgoing, and many people are shocked that I've ever been known as a shy person. But I've learned how to manage it so I can get out there and do what I need to do. When I have time to prepare for it, I'm actually quite social. But I need limits and buffers and escapes.

After a period of heavy socializing, I feel worn down, spent, drained of energy. Then I have to go be quiet for a long time. When I don't take this time to recharge, I get cranky, impatient, and eventually--sad and even depressed. I existed that way for years: constantly surrounded by people, constantly on the go, totally neglecting my need for solitude. The whole time, wondering why I was so miserable.

And then one day I realized that much of my anxiety came from not knowing how to take care of myself, not only as an introvert, but as a soulful person who needs to find meaning in things to feel content.

Instead of fighting against my nature, I started thinking about how to nurture it. I stopped calling myself crazy. That helped. I stopped apologizing for needing time to be alone with my thoughts. With an enlightened view of myself, I learned how to set boundaries without feeling uncertain or selfish.

I've come to accept that I will always be torn between my inner and outer worlds. I will always be slightly off the grid. Seeing things differently, experiencing things differently, stars in my eyes and fire in my bones. Crazy? No, not really.

I am a self-described wallflower exhibitionist. I like to stay in the background, but I want my work to be seen. I have a voice - I've worked hard to find it - and I want to make a difference. When I finally stopped resisting this truth, and gave myself the time alone that I craved, that is when I began to thrive.

If you are like me and you often feel overwhelmed by life, then you are reading the right book. You are not crazy or selfish or weird to value your solitude. It is important to protect your private time and preserve yourself. We all need that and I have learned that I need a lot more than I ever realized. There's nothing wrong with being sensitive, feeling things deeply and craving creative ways to express those feelings.

If you are like me, and you use your private time to connect with your inner world and make sense of things, then we are kindred spirits! You don't have to hide who you are or apologize.

But what if you are not quiet at all? Maybe you are naturally outgoing and expressive, but you keep your creative, sensitive side silent and hidden away, afraid of making yourself vulnerable. Fear doesn't care if you are an introvert or an extrovert. We all have to find the courage to overcome our insecurities and live authentically.

If you feel like your personality is holding you back, or like you have things to say but you are afraid to expose yourself, my intention with this book is to encourage you to build confidence and express yourself, without feeling obligated to behave unnaturally.

Just because you are quiet, does not mean that you don't want to be heard. Just because you are afraid, doesn't mean that you are weak. With prompts and insights to guide you, this book will help you peel back your layers to reveal your most fundamental fears and desires. With this awareness, you will be better positioned to channel your energy in meaningful ways and reveal the soulful, expressive woman that already lives within you.

"Within the souls of the awkward and the over-looked often burns something radiant."

— *Jo Ann Beard*

Sticks and Stones and Shy Beginnings.

I've always been shy and self-conscious, afraid of embarrassing myself. I cannot remember a time when I didn't feel this way.

I wanted to be perfect. I wanted to look perfect, fit in with everyone and never miss a beat. Say-all-the right-things perfect. Always-get-the-joke perfect. Cute-boys-like-me-cool-girls-want-to-be-my-friend perfect. I'm sure you know what I mean.

But I was shy. I knew that I couldn't please everyone, so I felt safest when I kept myself hidden and tucked away. I was sensitive and I thought that put me at a disadvantage. I thought popularity and acceptance would give me confidence and criticism would kill me - death by sticks and stones, too sensitive to tolerate a harsh word.

By the time I got to high school, I was an avid people-watcher. I studied before I befriended, avoiding aggressive, confrontational people. I became more outgoing over time, fueled by the attention of my carefully selected friends (true friends that I still have to this day). We weren't the most popular or the least cool; we were safely in the middle and generally liked.

They made me feel safe to be myself. They knew the real me and they loved me, helping me to love myself. When I was with them, I felt unthreatened and comfortable to be myself. Well, mostly.

You see, my mom has schizophrenia. She wasn't diagnosed at the time, but by high school I knew that something was not right with her. My friends knew that my mom was eccentric, and really, that's all I knew at the time too. At a time when all I wanted was to fit in and feel normal, I didn't know how to be real about my mother's behavior, so I hid it as best I could. I learned early on to hide things. I think we all do.

When we're young, we overestimate the gravity of other's opinions. If someone says something about us, it doesn't matter if we know it's not true, all that matters is that the person has put it out there and made us look bad. This is where it starts. Back then, I would give anything to not be talked about, to not be embarrassed. I cared what they thought and I didn't stop caring until much later in life.

A Wall of Limiting Beliefs.

"Safely in the middle and generally liked."

Maybe this worked in high school. But I carried this into adulthood. I was afraid to rock the boat; afraid to say how I really felt about things if I felt someone would disagree. I hated confrontation. I hated debate. I didn't like to stick up for myself because I wasn't sure about anything, like ever, so I didn't want to make myself look stupid. I was quiet. I liked being quiet. But I also felt limited by it.

Does any of this sound familiar?

Our fears box us into this little comfort zone where we feel safe from criticism, pain, failure, success, and risk. When we are in this zone, we hide our insecurities and along with that we hide our gifts and our creativity.

Maybe we don't think we have anything of value to add. When we feel shy, it is because we want to participate, but we are too afraid of what people will think and say.

I didn't think I was particularly creative back then. I did think I was pretty book smart until I got to college and started getting average grades. I thought I could dance until I tried out to dance professionally and was cut during the first round. I tried many things that I failed at miserably (in my mind anyway) and all of this served to prove to me that I wasn't that special. I was embarrassed about that, about not being special.

Forget wanting to be heard, I wanted to crawl under a rock and be average under there. Between my schizophrenic mother and thinking that I would lose my mind one day; and the pain of first love and first heartbreak; and then falling from grace so ungracefully with my education and career aspirations; I lost a great deal of the little bit of confidence that I had.

Without realizing it, I built up a wall of limiting beliefs within myself. A wall covered with things that I wasn't good enough to do, and dreams that I wasn't strong enough to believe in. I firmly planted myself in the middle of the road. "Safely in the middle and generally liked." I didn't want to say too much, work too hard, or be too passionate about anything. That would be too embarrassing and would expose me. Being creative was the furthest thing from my mind.

I had all of these myths programmed into my mind. Perhaps one of these will sound familiar:

You are too sensitive and you are incapable of emotionally handling the stress of being successful, or the stress of rejection.

Your natural preferences and interests are too eccentric and no one will ever understand you.

Criticism makes you look bad and diminishes your credibility.

Some people are creative, gifted and talented and some are not.

You need to play down your natural interests to make others who can't relate feel comfortable around you.

If something doesn't come naturally to you right away, then it can't be learned or eventually mastered.

If you try something once and it doesn't work out, then it wasn't meant to be.

It's selfish to make changes in your life that allow you to have more time to be alone and create.

You're a quitter, so you don't start things for fear that you won't finish.

You are creative but not strategic or business-minded, so you will fail if you pursue your passions professionally.

You don't like to network and promote yourself, so you are limited as to how you can express yourself.

Your happiness is dependent on other people, circumstances and luck.

You need others to approve of you in order for you to feel fulfilled.

Does any of this sound like you?

The constant, repeated affirmation of these kinds of thoughts becomes your self-prophecy. This is why it's so important to call out these fearful thoughts and explore them.

I didn't begin to question my thinking until much later in life. I started noticing things.

- People were always telling me that I had a way with words and that they felt such positive energy being around me. I made people feel comfortable and I accepted people where they were. Funny, I saved most of my negative thinking for myself.

- As I got older, I stopped doing things that I'd loved to do as a child. Sometimes when we feel that empty feeling, like something major is missing from our lives--and we think it is because we want a man or a child or a wedding or whatever--it is really because we don't have anything for ourselves, an outlet to feel purposeful about.

I didn't know it then, but I wanted to make a difference. There was something in me, a small flame that would flare up every time I wanted to give up on myself. It wouldn't let me. Beneath all the insecurities that I'd cultivated so painstakingly over the years, there was this purpose in there that wouldn't leave me alone until I found a way to satisfy it. Perhaps you know how that feels.

I'm Not Shy. I Just Don't Want to Talk.

I'm shy sometimes and I'm afraid often, but I wouldn't say that I'm a shy person overall. Not anymore. There's a huge difference between being shy and being quiet.

As I mentioned earlier, shyness is about fear. Quiet, however, is about instinct. Some of us are just naturally reflective and internal.

When I am quiet, I can process what I am seeing, hearing, and feeling. There was a time when my life was so filled with noise and chaos that I couldn't hear myself think. Most of what was swimming around in my head came from other people. I was always frantic. I had to go, go, go. Catch me if you can. When it was time to be still, I had to be high. That was how I coped with silence. I was too afraid to face it head on. Too afraid to face myself.

Since we all must deal with fear on some level, there comes a time when we must discern between the fear that can push us forward and the fear that can hold us back. The answers are already there inside of us if we only listen. It's called intuition.

But how can you allow your intuition to guide you if you are never still or quiet long enough to hear it?

Do you ever feel pressured to talk more than what feels natural? Have you ever been made to feel like you are being selfish or anti-social because you want to be alone? When you don't understand your need for solitude, these kinds of generalizations make you question yourself.

I used to feel inadequate when people would call me too quiet and dismiss me for not having more to say. It made me feel uninteresting. Now that I've learned to trust myself, I've noticed that I can be quite a blabber mouth when I'm talking to someone who makes me feel comfortable, particularly if we are talking about something I love. I mean, I can't shut up. Sometimes after conversations like this I feel bad because I feel like I was talking way too much and dominating the conversation. (Do you do that? After you've been out socializing or talking on the phone, do you review everything that happened and what was said and overanalyze all of it? Yeah, me too.)

Lately I don't mind if people make comments about me being so quiet or having nothing to say because I trust my gut feelings about who to open up to and when. If I feel that the people around me are not on my wavelength, then you can best believe that I won't say much. Alice Walker said, *"She was so quiet. So reflective. And she could erase herself, her spirit, with a swiftness that truly startled, when she knew the people around her could not respect it."*

I encourage you to do what you need to do to preserve your energy in the midst of your life's social demands. If you're at a party and you need to step away to be alone for a few minutes, then do so. If you need to choose one out of three possible social engagements for the week, that's fine, don't over extend yourself. See what I mean? In time, you will know when you really need time to yourself and when you are just afraid. Trust yourself.

The Sweetness of Solitude.

"Certain springs are tapped only when we are alone.
The artist knows he must be alone to create; the writer,
to work out his thoughts; the musician to compose;
the saint, to pray. But women need solitude in order
to find again the true essence of themselves."
— Anne Morrow Lindbergh

Only when I'm alone does the world make complete sense. Don't disturb this groove, I am finally at peace. Nothing needs to be justified. All is well or not well, and I get to decide. No one needs to understand me but me.

I get to take care of myself.

The comfort in my solitude inspires me, and I like to stay for a while. The hours feel like minutes, the weeks feel like days as I busy myself with self-searching, exploring and creating. My solitude is my glory, my heaven on earth.

There is nothing to explain. No one to tend to or put at ease. No one to teach or protect. During my time alone, I build confidence. I can understand the world by taking time to understand myself. So when tough moments come and I am challenged, I can make heartfelt decisions and live from this place of deep knowing.

Self-esteem is crucial to living a fulfilling life. You first have to believe that you deserve more happiness and less fear. If solitude brings you happiness, don't make excuses or apologize for it. If people don't understand, that doesn't mean it's wrong. Confidence comes from learning to nurture yourself, and setting boundaries.

When you don't honor your needs and preferences, you are allowing your state of mind to be determined by the outside world. You can't leave it up to other people to read your mind or set boundaries for you. Acceptance and appreciation feel good, but they shouldn't be your motivation for what you do.

How do you spend most of your time? If you are spending a great deal of your time feeling obligated and out of place, don't assume that it always has to be this way for you.

You deserve to do more of what makes you happy and create your own definition of success – regardless of the opinions of others.

For many years, I stopped doing two of the main things that made me feel most like myself. I stopped writing and I stopped reading. The guy I was dating at the time didn't enjoy either of these things. I immersed myself so much in trying to connect with him on his level that I left behind activities that were essential to maintaining my sense of self. Let me tell you, it's a miracle that I did not lose my mind trying to be what he wanted and clinging to him to "make" me happy, instead of clinging to myself and nurturing my own happiness.

Within this idea that I could be myself and love what I love and still be loveable, I began to see a glimmer of light.

When you make time for self-affirming activities that make you feel more like yourself, your life begins to change for the better. Things that once made you feel like an outsider will begin to be the building blocks of your authenticity. Don't be afraid to speak up and protect your time alone.

What Keeps You Up at Night?

Most people don't expect this question to come from a complete stranger. I get that. But this train of thought is more interesting to me than small talk about the weather. If we can't go beneath the surface just a little, then I'd rather not talk.

What drives you? What puts the fire in your bones? Do you have fire in your bones? Why not? What's missing? You look pretty, do you feel pretty? Why not?

These are the conversations that keep my interest. I like to swim in the deep end.

I seek the stories - context, layers, what makes you who you are. I crave soul connections and I'm drawn to creative, positive energy. I see it. I witness. I want you to know, I want everyone to know, that I see them.

Labels bore me. Titles mean nothing. A typical idealist, even facts are subjective to me. I have an aversion to absolutes, so I struggle to find significance where there is no tolerance for creative license.

If you could see into my brain, you'd find me always paying attention to the emotional currents in my environment like who was offended by a comment, who feels uncomfortable speaking but wants to be heard, who is being overbearing and needs to be buffered. Sometimes I'm so busy noticing the energy and the body language around me that I totally tune out the conversations. As a result, I often feel like I'm floating in a different world than everyone else.

Do you feel me yet?

Perhaps this is all quite self-centered. Truly, I don't feel obligated to partake in conversations and activities that don't inspire me, so I don't. I fly away inside my head. When you live in a world of your own creation where facts don't matter and souls are more obvious to you than bodies, you can become a bit of a snob. A messy, disorganized snob with unpaid bills and missed deadlines because you can't seem to come down out of the clouds long enough to pay attention to practical, technical things. Things most people care about, and that are necessary for the world to function.

But wait. How did I get lost in the climes of my own mind in the first place?

For a long time, I attached everything to categorical, tangible things. Everything was good or bad or black or white. Goodness brought heaven and sinfulness brought hell. Rich and poor were monetary measures. Success had a universal definition. These strict guidelines suddenly became insensible when my life became too complicated for absolutes and everything went from black-and-white to grey.

Schizophrenic mother. Poor grades in college. Pothead. Unplanned pregnancies. Debt. Bad credit. Grad school dropout. Unmarried. Unchristian. Unacceptable. Unlovable. Victim. Pushover. Loser. Underachiever.

Disappointments and burdens. Criticism and shame. These are the labels I carried around, tattooed on my insides, responsible for years of chronic pain and anxiety. While on the surface, I appeared as if nothing was wrong. My facts, when regarded without perspective, made me feel like a penny with a hole in it — hopeless — until I started telling myself a different story about my life, my gifts and what I once thought were my weaknesses.

You know, the things that keep me up at night.

And that's what puts the fire in my bones. That's what drives me. We aren't defined by where we grew up, or where we went to school, or what our parents did or didn't do, or anything else that happens *to* us or *because* of us. The facts we allow to empower or diminish us are merely the plot points in the real tales we need to tell.

Our real life stories happen in the less obvious, hidden places in our self-conscious where we are processing everything, deciding how we feel about it all and eventually creating an authentic response to them.

So I ask people about what keeps them up at night and what drives them and what makes them feel pretty because I want to know what stories they are telling themselves and on what facts or non-facts those stories are based.

I want to know who you are when no one is looking. The ups and downs that give you butterflies. I want to know what you think you have to hide but don't, just this once. I want to know the contrary part of you that doesn't want to be seen but craves attention, all at the same time.

So I can smile and say, I see you. *Do you see me?*

Anxiety.

Where did we get the idea that if we are too happy, something terrible is going to happen? We can't enjoy ourselves, can't let our guard down because we think that trying to control every little detail will protect us. We can't ward off disaster by being uptight.

Anxiety.

The telltale feeling in the pit of your stomach, the over-stimulation of your senses, the hyperactivity of your nerves, the paranoia.

The kind that lays dormant at times but never quite seems to go away. It hinders self-expression; corrupts imagination, and steals the moment. It can make you want to stay at home, not talk to people and not try new things. It traps you into a false comfort zone where you think you are safe, but the butterflies remain. You worry about what you're missing, and what people are saying about you. You worry that you'll never stop worrying. You wonder why you can't relax. Distress.

And what about the future? What about hope? Anxiety casts a dark shadow over any and everything that is unknown. You're always bracing for the worst, instead of expecting the best. If this is or has ever been part of your struggle, then you and I have something in common.

My young adulthood was rebellious and irresponsible. By the time I reached mid/late twenties I was a nervous wreck. I couldn't get into a car without envisioning the thing crashing. I could not leave my children anywhere for fear that they would get hurt in my absence. I checked my partner's text messages and emails every chance I got. I was constantly in financial turmoil with cutoff notices, harassing phone calls and overdraft fees. I was worried about everything all the time. All the while, I struggled to keep a cool, calm surface. I didn't want anyone to see the mess all piled up inside of me.

This was how I lived before I learned that I had choices. Anxiety is not the bully that we make it out to be. It's trying to give us physical and emotional red flags to draw our attention to a problem. Discomfort always comes with information, but we have to first realize that and then take the steps to translate it. If your car is making a strange noise, you take it to a mechanic to figure out why. If you have a headache, you eat, you drink, maybe go to the doctor, you try to figure out what your body needs in order to feel better. Likewise, if you're experiencing extreme anxiety, you need to know the cause of it so your soul can feel better.

You are stronger than you think. Consider all that you have overcome in your life. You've gotten through plenty of ugly situations with anxiety coursing through your body and you have proven to yourself that you *are* brave. Remember that everyone faces these moments. Everyone has these kinds of thoughts. You are not alone. No, you can't control or understand everything that happens in the world and there are plenty of things that will freak you out. There will be times when you will be overwhelmed and anxiety will build up against you, trying to scare you back into your corner of safe and familiar.

But if you think about anxiety as a form of communication, a signal that your body uses to get your attention, you can use your anxiety to become more self-aware. Get to the bottom of it. Look at it. Allow it to exist without being ruled by it.

You are your own mystery to unfold, so expect to surprise yourself. Expect to make mistakes and say unexpected things. If you are worried, channel it. Pray, write about it, draw a picture of it - do something with that energy other than allowing it to fester in your mind, struggling with it, turning the worry over and over. Transform it. It doesn't have to be a hopeless thing.

"Our anxiety does not empty tomorrow of its sorrows, but only empties today of its strengths."
— *Charles H. Spurgeon*

Are You an Over Thinker?

"Sometimes the best thing you can do is not think,
not wonder, not obsess. Just breathe and have faith
that everything will work out for the best."
– Author Unknown

As an artist, which is a very new title for me, I have to be vulnerable and put my work out there to be criticized. I cringe at the idea that I have to expose myself and grow in front of other people. But this comes with the territory. Even if you don't identify as an artist, you are a human being, and you are figuring out your life, one day at a time. So you are an artist and your life is your art. People will look at what you do with your life and based on their own perceptions, limitations and experiences, they may applaud you, criticize you or be completely indifferent. For many of us introverts, all of those three outcomes are equally horrifying!

I know the impact that I want to have on people and the audience I want to reach. But the execution part is extremely awkward. It's full of trial and error and embarrassing moments. It seems that playing safe would be easier, but that actually scares me more. For me, playing it safe means living a life that doesn't inspire me and wasting away my gifts.

If you're living your life to the fullest, you are often going to be faced with opportunities to take a chance and expand yourself. Being a beginner is not easy. We always want to be the best, right from the start, but that's not realistic. This is why so many of us quit or don't even start when we're presented with something new.

First, you have to know your special sauce. Then you must believe in it no matter what personal obstacles you have. What a shame it would be to look back and wonder what could have been. *If only I had stepped out of my comfort zone! If only I had spoken up or taken that risk!*

No failure or disappointment can ever match the regret of not giving yourself a chance. This is why we must build up a tolerance to being uncomfortable.

Your comfort zone should be a safe haven– not a place to hide. There's nothing better than coming home to a familiar place or activity after you've been stretching yourself to experience more. It only becomes a problem when we get trapped there.

I've watched myself create my own self-criticism and become painfully anxious based on what I *think* others are thinking about me. But we can't control what anyone else thinks, so it's a waste of energy to worry about it!

I might be wondering how my breath smells or if I have a booger in my nose, but I know that if I focus on those things, I'll become more and more visibly frazzled. I don't pretend to have it all figured out anymore. I'm gloriously human, a human who is very reflective, often awkward and lost in her feelings. If you are a naturally reserved person and you want to be heard, get ready to be uncomfortable often; but, with practice, you can learn how to exist in these moments and tolerate them graciously.

Don't aim for perfection; only strive to be as authentic as possible. You can stay true to your thoughtful nature and still express yourself. Always think about the possibilities, not the limitations.

What We Have is Much More Than They Can See.

"I had hoped to be disliked by most, not by way of rebellion, but by way of excellence, disdain for the habitual, and the common man's inability to grasp this. The act of being scorned? I saw it as a victory, my irreverent boast against this world which could never fully quench me."

— Coco J. Ginger

You may be organically quiet or shy, but you are not chained to a certain type of existence. You are free. Without realizing it, many of us are afraid of change because we don't know who to be outside of our current context. We wonder what people will think and who we will alienate.

Perhaps change is too strong of a word. What appears to be a change is really more like a reveal--a showing of the different sides of you. You don't have to always show just one side.

Some will understand and some will not, but the depths of your longing will only intensify if you suppress your desires. Trust me, it will just ebb and flow under the surface, making you feel like you are keeping a secret from the world that you were born to tell. What makes you different is your treasure. You can wear your jewels or keep them buried. It's your choice.

When I first starting blogging, I didn't want my peers and coworkers to know. My friends and family knew, but I didn't promote to anyone who knew me on a surface level. My writing was intimate and personal and I was so embarrassed for anyone who knew me casually to read about my deepest feelings.

But wait, why blog then, right? I could have just written in my journal or if I only wanted to share with people I was close to, I could have kept my blog private or used an email list. Something in me wanted to reach people. By opening myself up to strangers on the internet and showing all my colors, I learned that I wasn't alone at all. There were other women out there who shared my reflective nature and who craved inspiration like me.

Over time, I realized that I'd been taking baby steps toward aligning my external 'representative' with my true inner self. It became painful to go to work every day and go through the motions. I began to feel fake, pretending to care about the stock market and absolute returns and real estate. Pretending that my salary and bonuses made up for the cost of living an uninspired life.

I would sit in meetings pretending to take notes as I wrote down ideas for essays and blog posts. I would get an email from a gracious reader thanking me for being so transparent and for putting her feelings into words and I would feel more compensated by that than I would by my bi-monthly paycheck. I felt like I had a much broader calling than I ever realized. After twelve years of building a career in finance, I knew my days there were numbered.

What would everyone think? My friends, family and co-workers? They would think I was I crazy. An artist? Full-time? Yeah, OK. An entrepreneur? Remember all the other times you tried to sell things and you hated it? You have a good job and you are good at it. Don't be foolish and give up all the stability you have, especially when there are so many people in the world who would give anything to be in your shoes.

Once I got a taste of what it felt like to do fulfilling work, I knew I could not continue to devote 40 plus hours a week to meaningless work. I imagined what I could do, what I could create if I dedicated that much time to developing myself as a writer and creator. I began to accept the fact that I would have to surprise people, I would have to face the scrutiny and expose myself.

But the reward for that would be so sweet: I could finally be one person.

Not Corporate Gina by day, who talks the talk to pay the bills; and Creative GG by night, who hides behind her laptop sharing dreams and ideas. No, I would finally be one person, fully accepting what she loves and living it without shame.

This is for the Dreamer in You.

It's not easy to bare your soul for the whole wide world to see, especially when you are a naturally reserved person. But if you have the urge to create something, if you have a message and you want to share it, you can take small, steady steps towards finding your voice and using it.

Do you have ideas and philosophies, or a story of overcoming that you are afraid to share? Does your family disagree with how you live or decisions you've made? Have you ever tried to be something for someone and forgotten who you really are?

If you answered yes to any of these, I have to assume that deep down you want to be free of these limitations, but you don't know how. Any fear can be overcome and any mindset can be shifted if fueled with enough conviction. It will take a while to get used to putting yourself out there and sharing yourself, but it will feel wonderful at the same time. Here are just a few compelling reasons to take the risk:

- To gain a better understanding of what makes you tick so you can follow your bliss

- To attract people in your life who love you for the real you

- To attract opportunities that allow you to explore your natural talents.

- To inspire people around you to be themselves

- To accept yourself, flaws and all, and therefore be more accepting of others

- To be confident and not easily swayed

- To be consistent and sincere - not showing different faces to different people

- To be a leader

- To be self-driven and create your own experiences

- To free your mind from limitations that aren't real

- To be independent

- To reduce the impact of fear and anxiety in your life

- To be brave and vulnerable

- To be clear about what you truly want from life so you can receive it

- To stop comparing yourself to others

- To stop trying to explain yourself and start living the life you want

- To serve. You can't offer your gifts to the world if you are too busy hiding them

- To honor God. You were made the way you are for a reason. By being true to yourself, you are honoring your Creator.

Sometimes we visualize ourselves doing dream-worthy things with our lives, and we quickly talk ourselves out of them, citing all of these limitations and excuses as to why we can't make our visions come true. We take ourselves out of the game before we even try out for the team. I've changed my perspective on this completely.

I now live my life like I'm in constant preparation for all my dreams to come true. I feel the gratitude now. I feel the humility now. I feel the abundance now. I feel the dedication now. Whether I'm writing a blog with a handful of readers or writing a book with thousands of readers, I'm just thankful for the gift of writing and for the ability to connect with people through that gift.

The Most Awkward Girl in the Room.

"Even painfully shy and awkward people are not pain-fully shy or awkward when they are alone. The way to access this natural, comfortable alone-self when you are with others is by choosing to forbid yourself to wonder what "they" are thinking. Instead, force yourself to exist in the instant, then take it- and give it- as it comes."

— Augusten Burroughs

I'm not sure when it happened but at some point I realized that being quirky and unique was not a fate reserved only for a select few. We all are weird, but most of us try to hide it.

Your individuality is an advantage, not a liability. If this entire book could be summed up into one sentence - that would probably be it. You are who you are – the question is how can you shift your thinking so that your qualities empower you instead of impairing you?

Well, you don't have to do what everyone else is doing. I suspect that a lot of our awkwardness comes from trying to fit in and do what we think is expected of us. If everyone is talking and you don't have anything to say, don't feel obligated to talk. When I force myself to talk - I always say weird things that drive me crazy later. *Why did I say that? I hope no one took it the wrong way. Did I cut her off? Was I talking really loud? Did that sound stupid? Did I just spit on that guy?*

Whether you choose to be the life of the party or sit in the corner with a book, do it confidently knowing that it's exactly what you *want* to be doing.

Give yourself permission to laugh at yourself and own your socially awkward fumbles. You will feel much more comfortable and so will everyone else. Allow yourself the wiggle room to be a little left or right of center and be happy there. Laugh at yourself. Call yourself out. Learn to love the fool in you. As you do so, the people around you will pick up on this energy and many will follow suit.

The best thing you can do to make your complexity work for you is to know yourself intimately. When you know who you are, the things that make you unusual are the same things that also make you magical. You are confident and uncertain. Weak and strong. Straightforward and backwards. All of the above and none of the above.

Decide for yourself how you want to exist, how you want to feel and how you want to express yourself. Let yourself be vulnerable. Let the people who don't like it go, and let the people who do like it stay so you can build productive, authentic relationships. The kind of relationships that make you feel safe and beautiful and ironically, not the least bit awkward.

Mirror Mirror.

I've never liked my toes or my knees. I have my reasons. My arms and hands are so long that my fingertips are ridiculously close to reaching my knees when I stand with my hands at my sides. My forehead selfishly stole a good inch from my scalp that it really didn't need. I'm in my thirties, but I still have acne-prone skin. And somewhere inside there is still a 13 year old, insecure girl who wants bigger breasts, clearer skin and smaller feet. This little girl wills me to compare and contrast myself to other girls and wonder what it feels like to look different. She has internalized all the criticism that she has received over the years and now she finds fault in everything she sees, inside and out.

But in the last few years I have acquainted myself with another part of me that is spreading a different attitude and becoming the girl to watch among all the little girls that make up the woman that is me.

She challenges me to look at myself with loving eyes; she inspires me, and I believe in her. She speaks life into me and helps me to be less critical of myself and others every day. When she looks at me she sees all the things I've overcome. She sees the women who bore me and raised me and she sees the fruit of my own labor. She's teaching me to be more compassionate and to remember that we are all sensitive and human underneath our defenses.

Which voice are you listening to?

There's this woman that you spend all of your time with and no matter where you go or what you do, she comes with you and she talks to you. She could be your best friend or your worst enemy. That is completely up to you.

Listen closely. What is she saying?

Perhaps she fills your mind with empowering thoughts:

You are enough. You are loved. You are strong, purposeful, unstoppable, indefinable. You are free.

It's also possible that she weakens you with criticism and self-denial:

You are damaged. You are selfish. You make too many mistakes. You are a disappointment. Nothing you do is good enough.

Only you know what this inner woman is saying to you and only you have the power to change her tone. I still hear both voices clearly, but I've trained myself to ignore my inner critic. I don't feed into her negativity. I've learned to redirect my thoughts and believe in my highest vision for myself. It takes practice but it works.

Art Comes From Self-Discovery.

I used to walk around feeling like I was one mishap, one uncomfortable moment away from losing my mind. Things got better when I started writing. It helped me to sort out my thoughts and channel all that was inside of me into something that I could see, understand, and most importantly, share. Writing allowed me to express things that I couldn't say out loud. It made me realize that I didn't want to hide after all; I wanted to be heard.

We all crave connection. For many of us, there is something taboo about letting your guard down. Being vulnerable. Saying hey, I like to write or I like to make jewelry, would you like to see my work?

"But unless we are creators we are not fully alive. What do I mean by creators? Not only artists, whose acts of creation are the obvious ones of working with paint of clay or words. Creativity is a way of living life, no matter our vocation or how we earn our living. Creativity is not limited to the arts, or having some kind of important career."

— *Madeleine L'Engle*

What makes you feel good? What calms you? What makes you feel alive with purpose? Think back to when you were a child. I used to take tons of photos of my friends and family and I would put them in photo albums with sayings and quotes under each photo to create a certain mood and to capture the feelings from the pictures. I never would have guessed that habit would evolve into me using words and images later in life to inspire people outside of my circle, but that's exactly what happened.

My point is, don't judge what you love to do! Don't belittle it. Just do it and allow yourself to be comforted by it. Sometimes we run from things that feel good because we are afraid of joy. Yes! Afraid of joy! Imagine that, right? We are afraid of bright lights and happiness. Why? Because we are afraid of losing it all. If you find something that gives you life, indulge in it. Criticism and fear come with the territory, so brace yourself and keep going. Find strength in the fact that you are responsible for your own peace of mind and don't let anyone tell you what should make you happy.

Your Emotions Feed Your Creativity.

If you feel lost or you are struggling to find ways to express yourself, it might be because you are suppressing your instincts. Are you focusing on what you think people will like instead of what your heart is calling you to do? Are you beating yourself up when you think you've said or done the wrong thing? Are you forcing yourself into situations that don't inspire you and then wondering why you always want to flee?

Earlier I talked about stepping out of your comfort zone, but that does not mean that you should deny your natural instincts. If you feel sad, allow it. If you feel introspective, allow it. If you feel fear, by all means allow it, but recognize it for what it is. Is it the kind of fear that makes you tingle with curiosity? The kind that offers such a vivid possibility of happiness that it makes you feel embarrassed for even considering it? If so, follow that feeling! Push through it, and don't let it go!

Recently, I had one of those days where I was on an emotional roller coaster. I cried. I tingled with happiness. I turned things over and over again in my mind. I wrote a bit, which usually helps, but I had writer's block, so no release there. I was up and down all day. But I was quiet and I did my best to keep it to myself. I'm the quietest drama queen ever because I prefer to process my feelings before I share them, if I decide to share them at all.

I'm always processing. I get over-stimulated and I hide (classic introvert tendencies). When I'm surrounded by people and stimulus all day, it gets to me after a while. I get unbearably cranky when I don't get enough time by myself. I resent everything and everyone. I feel terrible about it, because I know that I'm closing myself off, but I can't help it. I feel mom guilt, friend guilt, you name it--it eats me up.

In the following quote, Rumi describes having a mob of I's inside.

In this mob of I's inside, which one is me? Hear me out. I know I'm wandering, but don't start putting a lid on this racket. No telling what I'll do then. Every moment I'm thrown by your story. One moment it's happy, and I'm singing. One moment it's sad, and I'm weeping. It turns bitter, and I pull away. But then you spill a little grace, and just like that, I'm all light. It's not so bad, this arrangement, actually.

— Rumi

I came across this quote in the middle of my reverie and I smiled to myself at how the right messages always find their way to me when I need them. This quote is so me. I'm a happy, sad girl. A nice, mean girl. An optimistic, incessant worrier who lives by faith and not by sight.

I came to this conclusion: Life is rich and complicated and every emotion we experience in the living of it is warranted. If you are able to channel your emotions into something productive, then by all means let your feelings ignite your creativity. And if you have not found that thing just yet, know that your emotions exist to help you learn about yourself and that's why you feel pain when you resist or ignore them.

Self-Promotion. The Good, The Bad and The Awkward.

I have a love/hate relationship with social networking and self-promotion. Like many other things, I tend to over think and feel self-conscious about it all. I love connecting with interesting people, but I hate the awkwardness of making random announcements and talking to any and everyone who will listen. That's not my usual method of operation, and that's essentially what I feel like I'm doing anytime I publish a blog post, update my twitter status or share a photo on Instagram.

Usually when I'm around people I don't know, I don't talk much unless I feel very compelled to speak up and add some perspective that I think is missing. I'm more of a watcher than a talker. So when I started feeling the urge to share my writing, I struggled to really promote it. It took all the courage I could muster to simply publish it in the first place.

If a quiet girl like me can face her fears of criticism, ridicule and indifference while soliciting faceless strangers to read her work and interact with her, then I know you can do whatever is necessary to attract your own opportunities.

How can you expect to find your people if you don't put yourself out there, telling people what you do and showing them how you do it?

That doesn't help, does it? Well, here's a thought. Focus on the message instead of focusing on yourself.

It's not about promoting yourself gratuitously for shallow reasons; it's about using the right platforms to promote ideas that matter to you.

> *"Self-promotion is the art of spreading ideas, concepts, and a greater vision. When you promote ideas, you give people something to cheer for... Your ideas might inspire hope, thought, or action . . . but as a general rule, good ideas inspire something."*
> *"* — Nathan Hangen

In order to become more confident and uninhibited about what you do, first think about what it's all for and how you can be of service through your message. Don't be discouraged if you build up your courage to promote and don't see immediate results.

There are some blogs that seem to blow up overnight. That has not been my experience. It has taken me a long time to build my following, and that has taken patience and diligence. I had to keep writing and writing and writing to find my voice and to find my people.

When I look back at some of my earliest writings and blogs, I feel so embarrassed because I was so green. But that is part of sharing your work as an artist. We have to evolve in public. We have to put out work knowing that we are still growing and that it will get better. My journey has taught me to be obsessively dedicated, to trust my instincts and to always be thankful for having an outlet that I believe in - one that gives me enough conviction to overcome my reservations and share my message with the world.

Imaginary False Artificial Me.

"We're so quick to cut away pieces of ourselves to
suit a particular relationship, a job, a circle of friends,
incessantly editing who we are until we fit in."
— Charles de Lint

How much time do you spend pretending?

I'm guilty. This almost exclusively happens when I'm in
on-the-spot situations, usually with people that I'm not
comfortable with. I never want to appear ignorant or un-
informed; especially if I think that the topic is something
that I *should* know about. So sometimes I pretend to know
things that I don't, or to be comfortable with things that
I'm not. But this kind of 'faking it' can lead to awkward
situations that are way more embarrassing than it would
have been to just admit the truth.

A lot of us temper our truths a bit in order to get by. We
pretend so we can cope. We pretend so we can fit in. We
pretend to avoid judgment. Sometimes, we pretend just for

fun. And other times we pretend because we don't know who we are.

Once you start pretending - telling a story about yourself that isn't completely true - you feel like you need to maintain that story, keep up the facade. As a result, you drain your energy, you feel anxiety, you worry about being found out, you run and hide. Who has time for that? It's much simpler to just be human and be okay with not knowing.

You don't have to explain yourself and for heaven's sake you do not need to fit in. We think that criticism makes us lose our power or credibility in some way, but of course, it doesn't. It's all in our minds.

We all like to be understood. I love talking to people who think like me and speak my language, but if I limited myself strictly to those interactions, I would never build up a tolerance to opposing views. My thinking would never be challenged. If you are certain, truly certain about who you are, you don't have to explain yourself to anyone. You won't need the validation. You will accept that everyone won't understand your journey, and you will fully embrace who you are and what you bring to the table.

Authenticity. It's like a built-in guarantee, but we don't realize it. It guarantees that we are always on the right track as long as we are being honest with ourselves and with the world about who we are and who we are not. Carl Rogers said, *"What you are is good enough if you would only be it openly."*

Envy, a Thief in The Night.

There is always enough beauty, love, happiness, success and talent to go around.

You know and I know that comparing ourselves to others is the thief of joy. But knowing something and applying it are two drastically different things. I really don't mean to do it, but it's like my mind has a mind of its own sometimes. Recently, I heard a quote from Rick Warren that really shifted my gears. He said, "Envy is saying '*I must be like you to be happy. I've got to look like you, I've got to have your money, I've got to have your kids, your family, your husband.*'" You fill in the blank. I've got to have your looks, your personality, your talent, your success, etc.

There's really no hope in that, you know? Why waste your life and your gifts by envying what someone else has? When my mind starts to turn on me and the grass starts looking greener, I remember the Rick Warren quote and it snaps me right back. So maybe I'm not super aggressive or outgoing. I don't always have the right words to say and sometimes I'm the last one to get the joke. It's okay. I am enough, just the way I am.

Instead of wallowing in self-pity, I use my emotions as fuel to continue on my own path. This shift in perception comes from understanding that things are not always what they seem. Why should I be distracted by romanticizing someone else's life, when I have my own life to live and lessons to learn? Sure, I still get jealous sometimes. But now I know how to interpret myself. I'm not a bad person who doesn't want to see others do well. On the contrary, I love to see others succeed; I just don't want to be left behind. The negative feelings come from my insecurity telling me that I can't keep up.

It helps to reflect on specific affirmations to change my train of thought.

I am worthy, capable, and destined to make a difference in the world.

Everyone's path is different. I can never miss out on what is meant for me.

I must set my own pace and I only need to keep up with myself.

There is more than enough love and abundance to go around.

I'm calm and determined and on the right track. All I have to do is keep going.

We don't have to worry about whether or not we will get a turn. Don't look at the next woman and wonder why she has what she has. Or, how is she such a mess yet still seems successful in her career. Or, why good things happen to everyone else but you. Don't believe any self-doubting thoughts that tell you that you don't have what it takes. Trust your own journey and breathe life into your own gifts.

The Hazards of Pointing Fingers.

There is something satisfying about seeing people make mistakes. It's not a pretty thing to say, but it's true. This is why celebrity gossip is such a moneymaker and the rumor mill is always buzzing.

People jump at the chance to criticize each other. Without an understanding of where this comes from, we find false comfort in taking our minds off our own problems and focusing our criticism elsewhere. Someone made a bad decision and is back in court. Yay! Someone made an album or a movie and their performance sucked. Burn! Retweet! We forget that these are real people, with real lives and all we are seeing is a snippet of their existence. We get caught up in what the media is selling us as news.

There is criticism everywhere. But it starts in our own heads.

We are already beating ourselves up about our own bad decisions. It's no wonder that we hide when we observe the harsh words and judgment all around us. When we are faced with challenges daily, we become afraid to put ourselves out there because we are afraid of how the world will judge us if we fail to deliver.

Since I started writing and taking more intentional risks in my life, I've become more sensitive to how I perceive others and the decisions they make. It takes a lot of courage to live boldly enough to risk making mistakes in front of people. People do the things they do because they are living out their own lives and the unique lessons they have to learn.

I've become kinder to myself which has allowed me to be more thoughtful towards others. I often refer to myself as clumsy and messy, not to talk down on myself but to acknowledge that I'm not afraid to look silly and be judged for my fumbles. I need those fumbles. I need my mistakes to make me better. We all do.

People will talk. But we must recognize our own lessons and find the blessing in them even if no one else does. Be selective with where you spend your energy! If you are often involved in bitter, negative conversations about other people, this energy will stay with you and poison your creative spirit. Without even realizing it, you will find your ideas blocked, your spirit affected by all the negativity. You'll be wondering, *What will they say about me? How will I handle criticism and rejection?*

I'm not saying that if you are a positive person that you will never encounter negativity, but if you are a positive person and you feed this energy consistently, you will be able to handle whatever comes your way without becoming jaded.

Rather than focusing on what "they" will say, hold on to what you have learned and remember how hurtful it felt to be criticized the next time you start to criticize someone else.

Misery Business.

Maybe I'm too sensitive. But I pretty much live by the standard that "If you don't have anything nice to say to someone, then don't say it." I prefer to just let people be who they are and do what they do unless it directly impacts me or mine in some way. I don't like when people give me unsolicited opinions about how I live my life, how I raise my children, how I dress, how I wear my hair. I suppose there's something to the whole "it's not *what* you say, it's *how* you say it" thing, but really no matter how you say it, if it's none of your business; it's just none of your business.

I don't understand it. Apparently, this is just how some folks operate. They must get some kind of satisfaction from hearing themselves talk. Or maybe they feel powerful when they think that they have successfully made someone else feel defensive or uncomfortable. You know the type.

It's toxic. We all have things we *could* complain or rant on about, right? But it's a slippery slope. I'm not saying that I never complain, but I always feel worse when I do. And when I'm around people who are always grumbling and speaking negativity into every situation they can (especially at work!), I want to run in the other direction.

Miserable people feed off the energy of others, and they'll take any kind of attention they can get. You don't have to allow this transfer of energy to occur. While you can't control what others say or do, you can control what you internalize. Keep your heart and mind clear of other people's trash. Know yourself, protect your peace of mind, and don't let them get in your head.

 I live for the idea that every unwelcomed event, person or situation is really a doorway into the next me. A stronger, wiser me. I'm always looking for the growth.

We get to choose. Don't allow factors outside of your control to drain your energy and steal your joy. Instead of waiting for people to change, you be the change.

> *"I will not let anyone walk through my*
> *mind with their dirty feet."*
> — *Mahatma Ghandi*

Stop Defending Yourself.

Want peace of mind? Let people think what they want.

I don't like to argue, debate or convince. All of those things are supreme vexations to my spirit, actually. Sometimes I stay quiet, simply because I don't want to trigger heated discussion. When I find myself getting annoyed because someone doesn't see things my way, I take a step back and settle back into myself.

Here's the thing. I'm all about sharing: ideas, concepts, projects, solutions, testimonies and stories. Everyone doesn't have to agree. But some people can't seem to share without arguing and attacking. I know there's a place for civilized debate, but it's just not my thing.

I feel free when I don't feel the need to make people agree with me in order to be solid in my truth. ✳

I particularly don't like to be questioned or challenged when it comes to my behavior. It feels like I'm being picked on, you know? Like, what's your point? Don't bother me.

For some reason I don't get defensive when it comes to tactical things, I guess because I'm not emotionally attached. But question my intentions? My creativity? Suddenly, I'm self-righteous.

I realize that I'm being immature. I'm acting like that girl, a younger version of myself, who doesn't know herself very well and feels threatened by any and everything. This girl needs to control what everyone thinks of her. She needs to have the last word. She needs to be right. She needs to be the victim, the innocent, the misunderstood. Anyone who has a problem with her or sees error in something she does is wrong and mean and she wants them to come away from the conversation knowing that. You're wrong, I'm right. And even when I'm wrong, I have my reasons, so I'm still right. So there.

Enough is enough.

The woman that I am now knows herself and has nothing to prove. I know that I can't control who I am to anyone else, but I can control who I am to myself. Why do I need to get all bent out of shape when someone says something to me that I don't like? When someone questions my behavior or intentions? My peace of mind should not be dependent on being understood by others. I mean, it's nice to be understood, but I don't want to need that approval in order to feel content with myself.

And what about accountability? What about growth?

Sometimes a person can say something that hits a nerve, an insecurity that we have yet to fully acknowledge; and because we haven't dealt with it, our reaction is super emotional and defensive. Deep down we know that there is truth in what they are saying and we don't like that they have brought up something that we don't want to deal with. *What?! You're mean, you're wrong, here's why. Now feel bad about yourself and apologize.* This is my ego talking to my imagined oppressors.

When I'm at my best, I'm calm and thoughtful and aware of my emotions without being a slave to them. I'm graceful in the midst of discomfort. I know that I always learn about myself from my relationships and interactions with people. If I'm secure with who I am, I should be able to hear both praise and criticism without taking off on an emotional roller coaster. I don't need to change anyone's mind about me. I can listen and reflect and decide what to do with the feedback I receive.

This is important to me because what I crave most is inner peace. I spent so much of my life only feeling peaceful when I was in good standing with others. So now, when someone makes a comment and I over think it and it steals my peace of mind, I feel that familiar angst that comes from playing the victim, having my peace stolen away, feeling unhappy because someone said or did something that wasn't part of my script.

When we release our need to control things, to be right and to be understood, we are also releasing the judgment of others. Do you ever feel like you are walking around constantly waiting to be judged? You don't want to speak up or talk to this person or get involved in this or that because you don't want to deal with people's reactions. When we surrender this judgment, we become free to be natural and peaceful without needing anyone's permission.

Habits of Soulful Women.

Strengths, weaknesses, preferences and idiosyncrasies. A soulful woman sees the beauty in her complexity and finds creative ways to express herself. If you are a quiet woman who wants to be heard, you must believe wholeheartedly in what you have to say.

Soulful beauty is about aligning the inner world with the outer world. Many of us retreat into our inner world and we find so much comfort there that we don't want to ever come out. I get that. But there are far too many compelling reasons to come out and share.

A soulful woman trusts that her natural instincts are relevant and shouldn't be devalued. She wants the foundation of her life to be based on spiritual things like love, peace, faith and creativity. She has a responsibility to connect with others and share her spirit.

Notice that I said nothing about being perfect. Perfection is the enemy of art and remember, your art is your life.

So if you think you need to be perfect, then you aren't really living, you are surviving. You are waiting for something to happen, for something to change in order for you to feel free.

You will keep wondering if you are doing the right thing, the socially acceptable thing. *Will I regret this? Will this cause me embarrassment? Will I be misunderstood?* This is perfectionist thinking.

We want to engage in soulful thinking, where the script is more like this: *No matter how this turns out, I'll learn from it. I know that if I don't take action, I'll always wonder what could have been. If I don't follow my heart, I will continue to deal with the anxiety of inaction.*

I'm not saying that you shouldn't consider all the scenarios and be thoughtful. But you don't need to have all the answers or all the solutions. What you need is self-knowledge -- a spiritual awareness that informs your decisions and directs you to fulfilling experiences. What's fulfilling for you may include stepping back or sideways or upside down before you step forward.

Mistakes are going to happen. But learning is going to happen too. That's where our creativity comes in. I love to remind myself that no matter what happens, it's better to know that you're at least in the game, putting yourself out there, going after what you want -- rather than sitting on the sidelines in a perpetual state of indecision.

 A soulful woman loves herself enough to trust her decisions and her ability to recover, no matter what happens.

Abusing Silence.

You know that part of you that wants to see the good in people? The rescuer? The one that sees the potential in dark places and the good intentions behind the bad decisions? You see people as puzzles just waiting for someone who has the patience to put them together. You are attracted to beautiful disasters. There's a 'fixer' in you that cannot leave a project untouched, whether it wants to be touched or not.

Have I hooked you yet, or am I just talking to myself? Hi, my name is GG and I am a recovering fixer/enabler. Let me explain how that works.

The Enabler. I've always been a comforter. Couldn't stand to have people around me who didn't feel at ease. So if getting high made them feel more comfortable -- so be it. If spending rent money on clothes temporarily made life feel livable -- okay, let's do it. Because I felt that if I needed a partner in crime for my own misguided escapades, I'd want the same understanding and cooperation.

The Fixer. I thought that love made people change. So even as I was enabling negative behavior by accepting it and partaking in it, I thought I was creating a bond that would somehow heal the person. I thought that since I could clearly see their problems, I could lead them to water and they'd gladly drink. All the while, I was actually hurting more than I was helping.

When you don't speak up and you get caught up in enabling people, you're stunting their growth. You can't do the work for them and you certainly can't buffer them from the discomfort that's necessary for sustainable change to occur. You are setting yourself up for a world of conflict and frustration.

I get it. I've lived it. And gradually I'm learning how to be more discerning and when appropriate, use my voice to speak truth into difficult situations instead of silently condoning destructive behavior. If you have similar tendencies, consider the following ways to start supporting people (and yourself) more constructively.

 Don't fall in love with potential. If you choose to get involved with someone, be sure that you love what they are and not what they could be.

 Remember that love is honest. Don't deny yourself or someone else the gift of honesty because you're afraid that it will shake them up or make them uncomfortable. Growth requires truth.

Let people evolve at their own pace. No one will change because of you. People grow, change, and evolve when driven by their own conviction. Period. No matter how much they love you, they must be self-motivated.

Don't compromise yourself. Set your boundaries. Love from a distance. Some parts of the journey must happen solo and without interference. You may feel guilty, it might hurt, but that doesn't mean it's not necessary.

It won't happen overnight. When you are accustomed to being passive and going with the flow (even when the flow is toxic), it takes a while to learn when to speak love into a situation, and when to walk away.

How to Be Yourself and Inspire People.

Spending all of our time seeking validation from each other slows us down.

I get so mad at myself when I'm supposed to be working, and I keep getting distracted, checking my social media accounts to see if anyone liked my status. Has anyone left a comment on my blog? Is anyone checking for me? Seeing what I'm up to? Checking, checking, checking. Someone rescue me from myself!

I am slowly learning how to share and do my thing without expecting something in return, without craving that validation and feedback all the time. As a creative person, I do love to connect and know that someone out there gets my work, but I don't want to allow praise or criticism to dictate how I feel about what I do. This dependency only diminishes the organic flow that is crucial for creative work.

Instead of giving ourselves fully to our own process, we are critical of others, we are critical of ourselves and we fill ourselves with doubt. *Am I popular enough? Do people like me? What am I doing wrong?*

The most valuable gift you can give to the world and to yourself is the natural, unequivocal you.

Believe in the beauty of your imagination. It's a gift, not a curse, not a waste of time.

Accept your humanity and your spirituality and don't be ashamed of either.

Don't worry about making people uncomfortable.

Indulge yourself in your music, your books, all the things that inspire you then go share all those good feelings.

Decide you are beautiful, without a mirror, without an appraisal, without validation.

Say what everyone is thinking but is afraid to say.

Say what you know everyone needs to hear to feel hope, to feel connected.

Smile mischievously when people call you weird. Weird is your escape from sameness and monotony.

Share your mistakes and what you've learned. Help others find meaning.

Show what makes you different. Show what turns you on.

Admit you are afraid.

Cultivate an idea and act on it. Put out what you desire to take in.

Keep going even when the going is slow and uncertain.

Make your dream your prayer and your service.

Don't wait for recognition. Let it find you working.

Romanticize authenticity instead of perfection.

Find Out for Yourself.

No matter how many warnings or opinions I receive, I always have to find out for myself. I have to do what feels right for me, even when my choices seem a bit reckless and illogical to others. It's a blessing and a curse.

It's a blessing because I make my own decisions and I know that I won't truly feel settled in a situation that I was forced into against my own judgment. But I also perceive it as a curse, because I'm stubborn and I often ignore good advice, putting myself through a lot of heartache as I'm trying to figure things out on my own. I annoy myself. I suppose we all do.

I want to do it all. If I could find a way to avoid sleeping altogether I would. I could put those hours towards something more productive! Time is one of life's currencies. We can't circumvent it, no matter how we try. What are we willing to give up in order to "have it all"? What is the cost and how do we ensure that we are using our time and our energy in ways that are meaningful for us?

We are living in a time when we have so much access to each other's lives. We see what everyone else is doing and we get distracted from what we are doing. Even if you know how to juggle, you will eventually start dropping balls if you are trying to juggle your own life and your own passions along with those of everyone else.

I'll tell you like I tell myself, stay in your own skin and experience life for yourself. What can you do right now? What is it you truly want at this time in your life? How much will it cost you and do you have the courage to pursue it no matter what anyone else thinks? Are you spending your time following your own bliss or doing what others tell you that you should be doing?

This is how I think about needs and wants.

Needs are mostly based on what we think we should be doing instead of what we want to do and how we want to feel. As such, these goals usually don't hold much meaning for us which leads to procrastination and guilt. These things probably make you feel like a responsible person, but you don't enjoy them, they feel like work. You do them because they are a necessary (but unappealing) part of some bigger thing you want to achieve.

When you find yourself lamenting about all the things you feel that you have to do, you have probably lost the connection between the task and the goal that it supports. You resent these tasks and you feel like this time is being stolen from you.

Periodically ask yourself: *Why am I doing this? How does this make me feel? Is it really necessary or am I falling into the habit of doing what others expect me to do? What soulful goal am I advancing through this task?* If you can't find any meaning in it, let it go. Many of us have restricting expectations about how much time we should spend cleaning, grooming ourselves, talking on the phone, etc. Challenge those things. Make sure they make sense for you.

When you recognize and reposition these things, you are making room for more authentic feelings and choices.

Wants tap into the heart and soul of who you are. They honor the things that you love about yourself *and* the things that make you feel special. These are your most honest, raw desires. You enjoy the process. You feel like yourself while doing these things. Your wants honor who you are, and not who anyone thinks you ought to be. They leave room for error. They feel good to your soul, even if they are scary. Wants won't leave you alone. When you don't attend to them, they distract you.

You want to write a book? You tell yourself all the reasons why you can't, all your responsibilities, you try to talk yourself out of it, but the desire remains. Listen to that persistent voice. You want to start a YouTube channel, start your own business, turn a hobby into a hustle that makes money? You don't need to know what will happen every step along the way. Believe and find out for yourself.

Don't over saturate your life by trying to live based on what everyone else wants.

Can you imagine? Not giving yourself a chance? Believing that everyone knows what's best for you, more than you do? Don't be afraid of mistakes. They will happen and still, you will be okay.

Take ownership. Feel the process, experience it, and remember it so you can one day tell the tale. *I dreamt this, I prayed this, I nurtured this, and I achieved this.*

She Won't Quit.

Quitting is not always the enemy. If you're letting go of something that is hindering you, then go ahead and quit. Let it go. Dismiss it and don't look back. It's fine to change your mind.

But if you find yourself quitting things that you really believe in, you've got to learn to trust the process and give yourself a chance. ✳✳

Especially if you are quitting because you don't want to draw attention to yourself. ✳

Isn't that the ongoing dilemma for us introverts? Wanting to share something with the world but we're afraid of being seen? Understand that you very well might fail the first time, the second time and maybe even the third time. You and me, we have to get over the fear of failure. The only sure way to fail is to never try.

If you constantly tell yourself, *I'm a quitter because I never finish anything I start.* Then you will continue to be a quitter. We must be so careful how we attach ourselves to deprecating labels and ideas. You need to fill your life with copious amounts of positive energy and affirmations in order to drown out the negativity.

You cannot successfully change anything about your life without first changing the way you think. There's a certain mindset that is required for personal growth, just like there is a mindset that reaps self-destructive and/or complacent behavior.

Our thoughts are like prayers. If you fill your mind with "CANTS", then that's what you will get. The way you replay your past in your mind and the way you process the present is affecting how you will make decisions for your future. For example, if you say, *I've always dated guys who are verbally abusive.* Then unless you start telling yourself that you *do not* date guys that are verbally abusive, guess what? That's exactly what you will attract and that's exactly who you will continue to date.

If you don't believe in yourself – that you don't have to settle and that you *can have* better – then you will continue to give up on yourself and accept less. If you don't value your instincts, you will continue to feel pulled here and there, overpowered by what everyone else expects of you.

How many times have you given up on something because it seemed too complicated? Not only have I given up, but sadly I can recall many times where I have not even started. We don't want to expose what we don't know, we are afraid of the risks, so we psyche ourselves out of the rewards.

I was equally afraid of success and failure for most of my adult years. I have sabotaged and talked myself out of so many things with destructive behavior and negative thinking. If I was trying to make an improvement in my life and I was making progress, I'd eventually start making excuses about why I could not move forward.

I had and still have a bad habit of comparing myself to other people, especially assertive people. Go-getters, people who speak their mind and get their way. People who are charismatic and always seem to have the right words to say. I convinced myself that because I am quiet and soft-spoken, I would always be limited. This is just another way to sabotage myself.

I have quit, I have sabotaged; I have searched for hope and destroyed it. We often do these things as we approach a certain threshold of success, because we become afraid. Our inner critic becomes louder than our inner guide and we unconsciously create obstacles so we can have an excuse to quit.

Sound familiar?

I know that you have goals and dreams. You can deny it, but we all have dreams that blow our minds with their audacity. We are embarrassed to admit them and we don't believe we deserve to actualize them. So sometimes we just have to fake it.

The whole idea is to exude the confidence of someone who already is doing what you set out to do or living the life you want to live. Act like, think like, talk like a version of yourself whose dream has already come true. Claim it. Fake it until it is real. This is how I get through new things. If I'm not feeling confident, I pretend that I am playing a character. The alternative – hiding behind shy and feeling stifled – is no longer an option.

So how do you push through your fear and your desire to quit and learn to fake it, without losing yourself?

Develop a relationship with the part of you that emerges (or hides) in new situations. What is she afraid of? What are her triggers? What motivates her? You will soon see that this is not about being fake at all, this is about understanding yourself and being intentional instead of being blindly reactive and giving in to fight or flight.

Find a reason, a soulful, heartfelt reason to push through, dig deep and find your own fierce alter ego: the part of you that has a mission and won't quit. ✳

What if No One Gets It?

Once you build up your courage and decide to speak up or put something creative out into the world, it may take a while for you to find people who understand - but they are out there. Never for a moment believe that you are the only one who feels the way you do. There will be days where you feel like you are all by yourself and people aren't responding to you. It will feel weird to keep pushing, but do it anyway.

The difference between being shy/insecure and being quiet/powerful is the conviction. You can be quiet and still persistent. Perhaps you don't talk as much or as loud as others, but your words are meaningful. Perhaps you communicate in other ways, through art or service. It doesn't matter, just speak. Find a way to express yourself.

The truth is that life will never be predictable. We can't expect everything to flow the way we want all the time. So, it's in our best interest to develop a tolerance for uncertainty and discomfort. Even when we know that we can't control a situation, we tend to stress over it anyway. The key to maintaining your peace of mind through the uncertainty is to let go of the outcomes and allow yourself to experience everything—ups and downs— without judgment. At first this may sound inconceivable, but if you think about it, this is what faith is all about. We must learn to trust that things are not always what they seem and that things will work out the way they are supposed to.

There will be awkward moments. When I published my first book, I felt like I might as well have posted a nude photo of myself online. That's how exposed and vulnerable I felt. I learned to sit with this discomfort and accept it. I taught myself that discomfort won't kill me and that eventually it will reward me. Only by revealing yourself can you make authentic connections and find the kindred souls who will inspire your journey. So even if at first you feel alone, don't stress, take a deep breath and keep going.

Our stress is often brought on by our own idiosyncrasies. We just can't seem to relax. We have so much to prove. Heroic acts must be performed. Many of us are so accustomed to drama that if we can't find it, we create it for ourselves. Is this you? Why not conserve your energy for what really, truly matters? Listen to your spirit and your body when it says to be still and recharge. Overlook small setbacks so you can be calm and centered for the big things.

When you encounter someone who wants to talk you out of your dream, or who always has something negative to say, don't lose your peace. It's no use trying to climb a mountain when you've got people all around you trying to pull you down. Sometimes our loyalty and attachments lead us to keep people in our lives that drain us and hold us back. We can't blame them, though. We can only blame ourselves for allowing them to stick around.

When you think about the things you want to do with your life and how people will respond to them, it helps to detach yourself a bit. Little by little, train your mind to care less about what others think and focus on the attention of your supporters, the people who feed your creative energy and give you life. When you write, picture yourself writing to them. When you draw, sing, share yourself--picture your ideal audience and how they will receive it. Trust that there are people out there who understand and who are on your side and if you stay positive and diligent, you will find them.

Intimate Discoveries.

Your Source.

What is the most important, can't-live-without thing in your world? Your God, your Values, your Faith in humanity? What keeps you from stealing and killing people or from jumping off a bridge? What makes you feel infinite and young and old, as if you've been here many times before? Your will to live and thrive has a source, and to live a fulfilling life, it is your business to know it with fiery certainty and not be ashamed to own it.

Your Inner Warrior.

How do you do courage? How do you do fear? Have you even discovered your inner warrior? The one that won't quit, who keeps overcoming, even when you think you've given up. The one who inspires others without realizing it, falling down and getting up, serving a purpose beyond your perception. You are stronger than you think and your fight is more meaningful when you share it.

Your Muse.

What inspires you to stay up all night and daydream all day? Wear it on your sleeve. Leave breadcrumbs so more of it can find you. Speak of it, write about it, sing it. Connect with your Source and seek out more of it. Challenge your Inner Warrior to be brave, go get your inspiration, trust it, create from it, and share it.

Your Sweet Spot.
Where do your talents and passions intersect? Knowledge meets Understanding meets Wisdom. Education meets Experience meets Purpose. Where does it all come together? Journey inside to this special place and see what it holds. Perhaps you have overlooked it or taken it for granted. Perhaps everyone sees it but you because it's so nestled in your core. Perhaps your Muse is waiting for you there.

Your Boundaries.
Where do you draw the line? How do you do self-preservation? Decide what stays out and what comes in and speak your truths. Trust your instincts and know what is real for you, what is worth sacrificing, and what you will allow. Package your life your way by letting go of the pieces that restrict you and fortifying the pieces that support you.

Your Dark Side.
What are your doubts, fears and weaknesses? Accepting them will calm you. Exploiting them will connect you and distance you and free you all at once. Forget the pretense and self-punishments. Your shadows exist to bring out your power to choose love. What energy will you feed?

Your Inner Beauty.

What do you love about yourself? Let the world see it in what you do, what you say and how you live. It is your gift, your duty to share and it cannot be taken away. Do not dim your light for anyone.

Your Paradox.

How do you contradict yourself? Acknowledge your complexity. You are a human and a soul, a fundamental contradiction. Don't try to be all one thing or hide yourself in rules. You deserve complete exploration. Rather than sit and wait for the world to tell you who you should be, get up and claim your right to find out for yourself.

It's Never Too Late.

I feel like I'm in the middle of a really good story. This is the part where the flawed but well-meaning main character is starting to trust herself. She's starting to believe that the life she wants is not out of reach or ridiculous or selfish or impossible. She's getting ready to embark on adventures and discoveries that will shake her up and blow her mind in new, inspiring ways.

Join me. Think of yourself as the protagonist in this story.

Just because you are quiet, doesn't mean that you don't want to be heard. It's never too late to embrace who you are and make your personality work for you. You don't need to wait, you don't need to fix yourself; you only need to BE. I hereby give you permission to stop waiting for everything to be perfect.

It's crucial for us to try new things and get over the fear of making mistakes – the sooner, the better. Get used to stepping out of your comfort zone so you can become an expert at handling unfamiliar situations. Too often we don't try new things because someone told us that they tried and it was difficult for them. You must form your own opinions based on your experience instead of relying on what others have told you.

You're not too old, your perspective does matter and what you don't know, you can learn. It's never too late to stop limiting yourself and start living a fulfilling life.

Everyone won't understand. You will alienate some, disconnect with others. But whatever is calling to you to come out of your shell and shine is worth the sacrifices that you will be called to make. What you want from life wants you too and there's no need to hide or diminish yourself.

There is no fairytale ending to this story. Ideally, the leading lady fulfills every vision she had for herself and goes above and beyond what she ever dared to dream--but not without stumbling blocks and complicated sub-plots along the way. This is real life. Avoid attaching yourself to specific outcomes and fixating on the actions of others to make your happiness achievable.

Ask yourself, *How do I want to feel?* Then fill the pages of your story with your experiences as you pursue those feelings. Instead of beating yourself up asking, *What's wrong with me?* Ask yourself, *What do I need to do; how should I be spending my time in order to feel good?*

When we make the connection between the activities that make us feel purposeful and in alignment with our true selves, we realize that our goals can reach beyond personal gain into a context that benefits our families, our communities and the world.

What larger force is your partner in finding meaning in your life? You can use any belief system or concept--secular or spiritual--that works for you, but in order to overcome old, self-defeating habits you need to believe in a larger force that will serve as your foundation as you're working toward your goal. This force will give you inspiration and strength when difficulties arise. Remember that the world needs your input and your voice matters.

NOTES.

You are your own mystery to unfold, so expect to surprise yourself. Expect to make mistakes and do unexpected things. If you are worried, channel it. Pray about it, write about it, draw a picture of it - do something with that energy other than allowing it to fester in your mind, struggling with it, turning the worry over and over. Transform it. Use the next few pages to capture the insights that come up from reading this book. You could write a letter of intention, detailing a few realistic changes you can make right now to move yourself forward. You can sketch or write a poem. Write quotes and affirmations that make you feel strong. Write about a day in your dream life, how you want to feel and what things you can do to begin to feel that way. Whatever you do, don't sensor yourself or write what feels safe. Go deeper.

_____

_____

_____

_____

_____

_____

_____

_____

_____

_____

_____

_____

GG Renee Hill is an independent author and blogger under the influence of three children and a passion for soulful living. She writes about all the many layers that make women the beautiful contradictions they are.

Find more of GG Renee's work and connect online:

Blog: www.allthemanylayers.com

Twitter: @ggreneewrites

Made in the USA
Middletown, DE
27 February 2015